No Gift for Greed

By RL Lane

The Gift...

Can you sing?

Can you dance?

Can you hold a pencil on your nose?

Whatever your gift is...whatever your talent...

It was never meant to be used for greed

For the pennies in your pocket

For the house with too many rooms

So you could walk around with your nose to the sky

Never looking down at the people around you...

He said something about how he's still hoping for the elderly lady to show up one day at the donation center where he works. He said he's still waiting for her to show up with her big bag of money that she'll hand to him and say, "Here take it all. I don't need it..."

Lenny is a wise man. I wonder why he thinks it will be a lady. Are women more generous than men?

I pulled up to the donation center one day with a load of items. Lenny told me I shouldn't be taking my car out like that. I should shine it up before I drive it around, he said. I don't have time for shining this car up I thought. I keep telling people I only have time to write and draw. Write and draw. Right…and draw. **Oh. The sword.** Draw the sword…

The sound of the metal as it was removed from its case

Metal

It seemed strong

My sister came across one recently

She said something about it being a sword from a group who had sworn off alcohol and all other bad things

 Oh.

The sword was strong. Like them.

They needed to be strong to live

An honorable life.

I could see Lenny as a knight. Standing there in his suit of armor. He would probably be the one directing the others. He would tell them straight up what to do to win.

Two swords. He would have one on each side. To slay all the dragons. The real ones. Not the imaginary ones. His helmet would be closed. His eyes peeking out. Oh. No. They wouldn't be peeking. They would be looking and watching. The leader of the knights cannot peak. He has to only look. But those suits of armor were so concealing. How could you even look clearly all around you? I wonder what it would be like to try one of those suits on. I would probably get tired just walking around with all that heavy weight. **Oh. The weight...**

It is true we carry around more than we should. Well, some of us carry around more than we should. Others cast off the weight because they cannot carry it or do not want to carry it…

Some carry it for two

Some never get the chance to

carry the weight

Some never see the chance to

carry the weight.

Carry

The weight.

I love that this story has all these poems. I wasn't expecting it to have so many. I hope Lenny likes poems.

I really do think that is how it is supposed to be. No gift for greed. Maybe it is better for people to rise to fame when they are older. *Tomorrow is my birthday. I will be 45. It seems like just yesterday that I was writing that I had reached the half point of my life, but now it is already years past.* Maybe it is harder for the younger generation to not be tempted by the riches of life. The fake riches of life. **Oh. The riches…**

The real ones don't cost a penny

I know that because I remember the cavemen

They had no money

They slept in caves I think

Or maybe when it was nice out they just slept in the grass

Under the sky

They didn't eat their dinners served on platters

They didn't even serve their food

They were dirty

There was no perfume to hide their dirt.

They had a lot of dirt.

See.

We aren't that different from our cavemen fathers.

Oh. The fathers. Did they have to do it all even way back then? They were the hunters. The providers. Well, the women had to birth the babies. I think they cleaned the caves. They had to protect the children when the men were out hunting. They had to shelter them at night. Did they really howl at the moon? **Oh. The moon...**

Don't forget to look up each night.

Unless there are clouds

You will not see the moon

Or if it is a new moon

It won't be there

Well it will be there

You just won't see it

But you can believe

It is still there.

I wonder what the cave people thought about the moon.

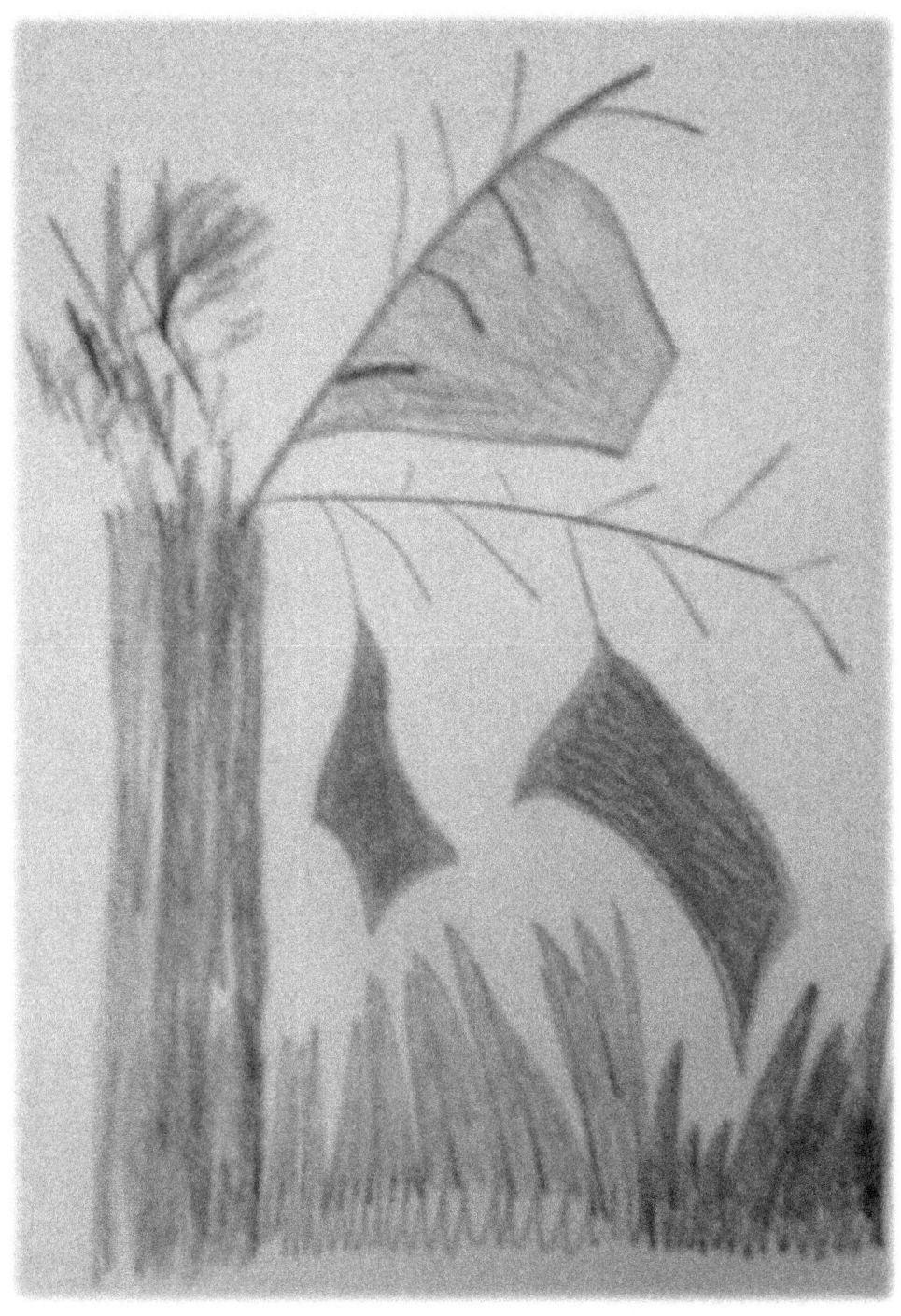

I left that as the only picture in this book. I think it is such an honorable picture. The flag staked in the tree with two red flags hanging low. The red flags to wave the bull on...to take charge...

It is funny that gift is in the title, since tomorrow is my birthday. I do hope I get a gift. It does not have to be one bought with money. It could be a stick. **Oh. The stick…**

From the tree

The trees that they both loved

Eden Eddy and My Dad…Mr. Wig

The writer and the writer

They did both love to write

He loved poems

Eden Eddy…

My Dad's brother

Oh. The sword.

Oh. The weight.

Oh. The riches.

Oh. The moon.

Oh. The stich…stitch…stick.

That's funny. I texted my brother recently that I had a dream about him and chicken bones and stitches. You can imagine my family gets a lot of odd messages from me.

The sword that slayed the dragon.

The riches that slayed the people.

The weight that slayed the man.

The moon that slayed the…

The stick.

The stick that beat the man?

Why would you use a stick to hit anyone?

The stick that grew from the tree of life?

My brother poked me in the eye once with a stick when we were kids, but it was just an accident. We would talk about it from time to time. Oh wait. Maybe it was just my nose that he hit. I don't remember needing stitches or anything.

Greed – excessive desire for wealth or possessions.

That is how it is defined, but what is excessive? Who defines what is excessive? Is fourteen bedrooms excessive? Is it ok to have a house with fourteen bedrooms if a homeless man is staying in each one? What if the rooms just sit there empty? They do give the cleaning people more work to do. That means more money in their pockets.

I talked to Darryl about this book while I was still writing it. He said people work hard for their money and no one should tell them how to spend it. It made me think of all the people working hard for their money…the ones who have two or three jobs just to get by. They work hard yet they still have no money. My Mom worked hard all her life but had no money. Did she and the others not find their gift? Every gift can't mean wealth and prosperity to everyone. Any starving artist can tell you that.

Darryl says he has a lot of fishing gear. He loves to fish. It made me think of my Dad. He was dirt poor till the day he died. He used to dig in the dirt to get his bait. Looking for the worms after the rain. I have no doubt he loved to fish as much as Darryl does. Maybe Darryl catches more fish with his big variety of lures and bait. I have no doubt. My Dad had no luck in getting those fish to take the bait.

The real message of this story. *"Here take it all. I don't need it..."*

It shouldn't be your final message before you leave this rock.

I have to write these words so when RL Lane gets there I can carry this book as a reminder...

No Gift for Greed.

About the Author and *Illustrator*

RL Lane has published the EcarreT series and a collection of short stories featuring the author's illustrations throughout the books. The series begins with "Chapel Street Signs"…

...unexplained connections that challenge us to beli ve. A woman, a Dad a Doctor, a cat and mouse, a horse and tale tell their stories. "Do you beli ve in spirits?" I asked my friend. "Well look", he said, "I believe there are things that cannot be explained..." Oh. Plus, hear ov a Mom's battle with her struggle to connect to the woman...her little girl.

Welcome to EcarreT...a world
Where everyone cares
Why did I have to create it in...

A fiction fantasy world?

You may already know why, but you will see regardless of what you believe as a girl's journey of love and faith on her "Touring Machine" take her on the best journey of her mundane life. A life well on its way takes a turn in a direction that could've never been seen or even dreamed...

The author can be contacted at:

RosaLeeeLane@gmail.com
www.Amazon.com/author/readrllane

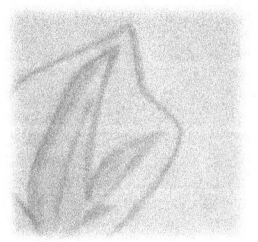

ISBN: 1517316987
ISBN-13: 978-1517316983